FREEDOM IN CHRIST

NEIL T. ANDERSON & STEVE GOSS

Participant's Guide

A 13 WEEK DISCIPLESHIP COURSE FOR EVERY CHRISTIAN

FULLY REVISED AND UPDATED EDITION

MONARCH
BOOKS

Oxford, UK & Grand Rapids, Michigan, USA

Published by Monarch Books
an imprint of
Lion Hudson plc
Wilkinson House, Jordan Hill Road,
Oxford OX2 8DR, England
Email: monarch@lionhudson.com
www.lionhudson.com/monarch

ISBN: 978-1-85424-940-1
ISBN: 978-1-85424-941-8 (pack of five)

First edition 2004. This edition 2009.

Acknowledgments
Unless otherwise stated, Scripture quotations are taken from the Holy Bible, New International Version, © 1973, 1978, 1984 by the International Bible Society. Used by permission of Hodder & Stoughton Ltd. All rights reserved.

A catalogue record for this book is available from the British Library.

Printed and bound in the UK, April 2015, LH26

Contents

Comments From Previous Participants On The Freedom In Christ Course

"I have a clear head, praise Jesus — it's not been really clear for years!"

"Knowing who I am in Christ and accepting the truth of God while rejecting the lies of the devil has changed my life."

"It is helping me to grow and mature as a Christian as never before."

"My life has been transformed. It truly was like walking from darkness back into light again."

"I was separated from the truth of God's love and Jesus' liberation by a large wall of pain, wounds and lies. But the wall came tumbling down."

"It proved to be a pivotal point in my Christian life... I now feel that I have the abundant life which Christ spoke of and which I have been yearning for."

Why Take Part In This Course?

The Freedom In Christ course is for every Christian, from those who have been Christians for a long time to those who have only just made that decision, from those who are progressing steadily to those who feel stuck.

It is designed to help you:

- **break through to a greater level of spiritual maturity**
- **uncover any areas of deception holding you back**
- **resolve personal and spiritual conflicts**
- **learn strategies to renew your mind and break free from negative thinking and unhelpful patterns of behaviour**

The course does not focus on how to behave but on how to believe. After all, Christ has already set us free (Galatians 5:1) and given us everything we need (2 Peter 1:3). It's just that sometimes it doesn't feel like it!

Many sense that they have not reached their full potential for God. Perhaps they feel "stuck" in habitual sin, negative thoughts, fears, unforgiveness or condemnation. Yet they really want to grow and mature. This course will help you grasp the amazing truth of your new identity in Christ, teach you to uncover and resist the enemy's deception, and help you move on. It's not a "quick fix". But it is likely to revolutionise your Christian life.

How Can I Get The Most Out Of It?

Do your best to get to each session.

Read the accompanying books (see page 6) or **Victory Over The Darkness** and **The Bondage Breaker** by Neil Anderson to reinforce the teaching.

Use the 'In The Coming Week' suggestions at the end of each session.

Ensure you go through The Steps To Freedom In Christ, a kind and gentle process during which you ask the Holy Spirit to show you any areas of your life where you may need to repent. Most churches schedule this between Sessions 9 and 10 and for many it is a life-changing experience.

The course includes strategies for standing firm in the freedom won and renewing your mind on an ongoing basis — make them part of daily life.

Get More Out Of The Course

Steve Goss has written four slim, easy-to-digest books specifically for participants on the Freedom In Christ course. They present the same teaching but in a different way with additional material so that you can take the message deeper. They cost £5.99 each or £19.95 for all four (plus £3 p&p). Available from **www.ficm.org.uk** or by calling **0118 321 8084**. They are also widely available through Christian bookshops.

Free to be Yourself — Enjoy your true nature in Christ. Many Christians act as they think a Christian should act — and find that they simply can't keep it up. They either drop out or burn out. True fruitfulness comes from realising that we became someone completely new the moment we became Christians. **Corresponds to Part A (Sessions 1 to 3).**

Win the Daily Battle — Resist and stand firm. You are in a raging battle, whether you like it or not. Your only choice is to stand and fight or to become a casualty. Arrayed against you are the world, the devil and the flesh but once you understand how they work and just who you are in Christ, you can expect to emerge victorious from every skirmish with them. **Corresponds to Part B (Sessions 4 to 7).**

Break Free, Stay Free — Don't let the past hold you back. Every Christian has a past. It can hold us back big-time. Those of us with a lot of "stuff" know that only too well. But even those who have had a relatively trouble-free existence need to know how to resolve negative influences that stop us moving on. **Corresponds to Part C (Sessions 8 to 10 — part).**

The You God Planned — Don't let anything hold you back! Once we have claimed our freedom in Christ, how do we remain in it and make fruitfulness a way of life? How do we know what God is calling us to be anyway? Are the goals we have for our lives in line with His goals? How can we stop others getting in the way? And how do we avoid getting in their way? **Corresponds to Part D (sessions 10 — part — to 13).**

SESSION 0: Introduction

INTRODUCTION

This session is an optional introduction to the Freedom In Christ course.

 WELCOME

What is the best book you have ever read (apart from the Bible)?

 WORSHIP

Putting God right at the centre of the course and opening our hearts to Him. Jeremiah 29:11-13, Psalm 33:4-7, Hebrews 4:12, Philippians 1:6.

 WORD

Focus verse: For the word of God is living and active. Sharper than any double-edged sword, it penetrates even to dividing soul and spirit, joints and marrow; it judges the thoughts and attitudes of the heart. (Hebrews 4:12)

Focus truth: When it comes to books, the Bible is in a league of its own and there are several very good reasons for believing that it is God's message to the people He created.

What Is Freedom In Christ All About?

Jesus told his followers to go into all the world and 'make disciples' (see Mark 16:15, Matthew 28: 19).

A disciple is not the same thing as a 'convert' or 'someone who believes'. It's someone who is learning continually.

It's not about head knowledge. It's about getting to know a real person — Jesus — better and better and seeing the effects of that work out in our lives.

PAUSE FOR THOUGHT 1

What is the best bit of advice you've ever been given?

If you needed some really important advice and asked different people for it and they gave you different opinions, how would you decide which to trust?

Can you think of any times you were given misleading information by someone? What happened?

Why Should We Trust The Bible?

The Bible is easily the most influential book ever written:

- it was the first book ever printed
- it has been translated into over 2,500 languages
- it contains over 750,000 words
- it would take you about 70 hours to read the whole Bible out loud.

Even though it was written by 40 different people (from kings to fishermen) who lived over a period of 1,500 years on three continents, the great claim of the Bible is that, taken together as a whole, it is the message of God Himself to the people He created. To quote the Bible itself, "All Scripture is breathed out by God." (2 Timothy 3:16). But why should we trust it?

1. History Confirms The Bible

To date, the findings of archaeology have done nothing except verify the Bible's historical accuracy.

If the Bible is proved accurate in its historical detail, it's a strong reason for giving serious consideration to the things it reports that may seem out of the ordinary or impossible.

Note: there are many books you can read to confirm this and other points made in this session. Your group leader will be able to recommend some.

2. What The Bible Said Would Happen Did Happen

The Bible is full of predictions about the future (prophecies) that came true, many of which seemed extremely unlikely to happen.

Many details of the life and death of Jesus Christ were written down accurately hundreds of years before His birth.

3. The Bible's Claim That Jesus Rose From The Dead Is Credible

This is a startling claim but the evidence supports it. Those who were there clearly believed it as many of them went on to die for that belief.

4. The Church Has Never Stopped Growing

The Church took until 1900 to reach 2.5% of the world population. Then, in just 70 years it doubled to reach 5%. In the next 30 years — between 1970 and 2000 — it more than doubled again to reach 11.2%.

The decline in the Church in the West is a historical anomaly that is far outweighed by the growth elsewhere.

 WITNESS

If someone told you that they thought the Bible was "just a collection of myths and legends" what would you say to them?

 IN THE COMING WEEK

If you have never got to grips with reading the Bible regularly before, why not try reading a little bit each day? You could start with one of the Gospels, Matthew, Mark, Luke or John. As you read, remind yourself of the truths we have looked at and that the Creator of the universe wants to speak to you today through His Word, the Bible. Wow!

SESSION 1: Where Did I Come From?

PART A — KEY TRUTHS

Jesus said that we will know the truth and the truth will set us free! In the first three sessions we look at some of the key truths we need to know about what it means to be a Christian.

WELCOME

Spend a couple of minutes in pairs finding out as much as you can about each other. Then, in no more than 30 seconds, answer this question about your partner. "Who is he/she?"

WORSHIP

God's plans and promises. Psalm 33:10-11, Job 42:2, Proverbs 19:21.

WORD

Focus verse: He who has the Son has life; he who does not have the Son of God does not have life. (1 John 5:12)

Focus truth: Before we became Christians, we were driven by the need to be accepted, secure and significant. Now, in Christ, we are spiritually alive children of God who are accepted, secure and significant.

Who Are You Really?

What makes up the real "me"? Is it my body? Is it what I have? Is it what I do? Is it what I think?

You Are Created In The Image Of God (Genesis 1:26)

God is Spirit and we too have a spiritual nature, an inner person (or soul/spirit). It is not our outer person (our body) that is created in the image of God; it's our inner person that has the capacity to think, feel and choose.

How We Were Designed To Be

Physically Alive
Our spirit connected to our body

Spiritually Alive
Our spirit connected to God

Being spiritually alive and connected to God meant that Adam and Eve possessed a number of very important qualities of life:

1. Significance

2. Security

3. Acceptance

That's how God created you to be: a real purpose; absolute security; and a sense of belonging to God and to other people.

PAUSE FOR THOUGHT 1

If you feel able to do so, could you say why you came on the course and what you hope to get from it?

Imagine Adam and Eve's daily life as they were originally created. How would it have been different to yours?

What do you think they would have thought about as they dropped off to sleep each night?

The Consequence Of The Fall

Spiritual Death

The effects of Adam and Eve's sin can be summed up by one word: "death". Some of the effects of this spiritual death for them (and consequently for us) were:

1. Lost knowledge of God

"They are darkened in their understanding and separated from the life of God because of the ignorance that is in them due to the hardening of their hearts" (Ephesians 4:18).

2. Negative emotions

They felt:

- fearful and anxious
- guilty and ashamed
- rejected
- weak and powerless
- depressed and angry

Trying To Go Back To How It Was Meant To Be

The Best The World Can Offer Does Not Work

The world offers us a number of false equations which it promises will recover what Adam and Eve lost:

Performance + Accomplishments = Significance

Status + Recognition = Security

Appearance + Admiration = Acceptance

"Utterly meaningless! Everything is meaningless." (Ecclesiastes 1:2)

Obeying Rules Does Not Work

God gave the Law to His people but it was powerless to restore the life that Adam and Eve lost. It was intended to make us aware of the utter hopelessness of our situation and point us to Christ, the ultimate sacrifice for sin.

PAUSE FOR THOUGHT 2

What were the consequences of Adam and Eve's sin for us?

Which ones do you particularly identify with and why?

Look at the 'Best The World Can Offer' false equations on page 14. How do people generally try to deal with their strong needs to feel significant, secure and accepted? Try to give specific examples that you have experienced yourself or observed in others.

What Jesus Came To Do

Give Us Back Spiritual Life

The only possible answer to our predicament was to restore our relationship with God, to reconnect our spirit to God's Spirit so that we could become spiritually alive again.

"I have come that they may have **life**, and have it to the full" (John 10:10). (Our emphasis)

"In the beginning was the Word... In him was **life**, and that **life** was the light of men" (John 1:1-4). (Our emphasis)

"I am the resurrection and the **life**. He who believes in me will **live**, even though he dies" (John 11:25). (Our emphasis)

What Adam lost was **life**. What Jesus came to give us was **life**.

Restore Significance, Security And Acceptance

Did you think that eternal life is something that you get when you die? It's much more than that — it's a whole different quality of life **right now**.

"He who has the Son has life; he who does not have the Son does not have life" (1 John 5:12).

Now our needs to establish an identity, to be accepted, secure and significant can be fully met in Christ.

PAUSE FOR THOUGHT 3

Of the statements we read out together, were there any that surprised you? Why?

Of the statements we read out together, which ones particularly encouraged you? Why?

If God says something about us but it doesn't feel true to us, how can we respond to it?

 WITNESS

How do people generally try to deal with their strong need to feel accepted, significant and secure? How would you explain to a non-Christian neighbour that ultimately these are found only in Christ?

 IN THE COMING WEEK

Read the "Significance, Security & Acceptance Restored In Christ" list out loud every day. Then pick one of the truths that is particularly relevant to you and spend some time reading it in its context and asking God to help you understand it more fully.

I Am Significant

I am no longer worthless, inadequate, helpless or hopeless. In Christ I am deeply significant and special. God says:

Matthew 5:13,14	I am the salt of the earth and the light of the world.
John 15:1,5	I am a branch of the true vine, Jesus, a channel of His life.
John 15:16	I have been chosen and appointed by God to bear fruit.
Acts 1:8	I am a personal, Spirit-empowered witness of Christ.
1 Corinthians 3:16	I am a temple of God.
2 Corinthians 5:17-21	I am a minister of reconciliation for God.
2 Corinthians 6:1	I am God's fellow worker.
Ephesians 2:6	I am seated with Christ in the heavenly realms.
Ephesians 2:10	I am God's workmanship, created for good works.
Ephesians 3:12	I may approach God with freedom and confidence.
Philippians 4:13	I can do all things through Christ who strengthens me!

I Am Secure

I am no longer guilty, unprotected, alone or abandoned. In Christ I am totally secure. God says:

Romans 8:1,2	I am free forever from condemnation.
Romans 8:28	I am assured that all things work together for good.

Romans 8:31-34	I am free from any condemning charges against me.
Romans 8:35-39	I cannot be separated from the love of God.
2 Corinthians 1:21,22	I have been established, anointed and sealed by God.
Philippians 1:6	I am confident that the good work God has begun in me will be perfected.
Philippians 3:20	I am a citizen of heaven.
Colossians 3:3	I am hidden with Christ in God.
2 Timothy 1:7	I have not been given a spirit of fear, but of power, love and a sound mind.
Hebrews 4:16	I can find grace and mercy to help in time of need.
1 John 5:18	I am born of God and the evil one cannot touch me.

I Am Accepted

I am no longer rejected, unloved or dirty. In Christ I am completely accepted. God says:

John 1:12	I am God's child.
John 15:15	I am Christ's friend.
Romans 5:1	I have been justified.
1 Corinthians 6:17	I am united with the Lord and I am one spirit with Him.
1 Corinthians 6:19,20	I have been bought with a price. I belong to God.
1 Corinthians 12:27	I am a member of Christ's Body.
Ephesians 1:1	I am a saint, a holy one.
Ephesians 1:5	I have been adopted as God's child.
Ephesians 2:18	I have direct access to God through the Holy Spirit.
Colossians 1:14	I have been redeemed and forgiven for all my sins.
Colossians 2:10	I am complete in Christ.

SESSION 2: Who Am I Now?

WELCOME

Imagine you are talking to a not-yet Christian. Can you summarise the gospel message in a sentence or two?

Or: How was the gospel message explained to you when you became a Christian?

WORSHIP

Realising just how much God loves us and delights in us. Ephesians 3:16-19, Zephaniah 3:17, 2 Corinthians 3:18, Hebrews 12:1-2, Psalm 103:8-17.

WORD

Focus verse: If anyone is in Christ, he is a new creation; the old has gone, the new has come! (2 Corinthians 5:17)

Focus truth: Your decision to follow Christ was the defining moment of your life and led to a complete change in who you now are.

Who Am I Now?

At one time, "we were by nature objects of wrath" (Ephesians 2:3).

The moment you became a Christian was the defining moment of your life. Everything changed. Take careful note of the tenses used in the following verses:

"If anyone is in Christ, he is a new creation; the old has gone, the new has come!" (2 Corinthians 5:17) Can you be partly old creation and partly new?

"For you were once darkness, but now you are light in the Lord." (Ephesians 5:8) Can you be partly darkness and partly light?

"He has rescued us from the dominion of darkness and brought us into the kingdom of the Son he loves." (Colossians 1:13) Can you be in both kingdoms?

A Saint — Not A Sinner

"While we were still sinners, Christ died for us" (Romans 5:8). If our fundamental identity is no longer that of a "sinner", what are we?

In the New Testament, the word "sinner" is used (over 300 times) to refer to unbelievers. Believers, on the other hand, are identified (over 200 times) as "saints". The word "saint" means "a holy one" or "someone who is righteous".

Even the youngest Christian is a saint.

We are saints not because of our own goodness or what we have done but because of our new identity and position "in Christ".

Not Just Forgiven But A Whole New Person

Changed Behaviour Comes From Realising You Are A Whole New Person

If you think of yourself as a forgiven sinner (but still a sinner), what are you likely to do? Sin! If you want to change your behaviour you have to see yourself as more than just forgiven.

If you came across a dead man and you wanted to save him, you would have to:

1. Work out how to cure the disease that caused him to die (in our case, sin).
2. Give him life again.

If we knew only that Jesus died to cure the problem of sin, we would believe that we were forgiven sinners. Knowing the truth that we have also received back the life that Adam lost and become saints is crucial if we want to live a life that honours God.

Defeat Comes From Not Realising You Are A Whole New Person

Satan can't do anything to change that historical fact of who you now are but if he can get you to believe a lie about who you are, he can cripple your walk with the Lord.

You are not saved by how you **behave** but by how you **believe**.

Being Pleasing To God

What Happens When We Go Wrong?

The problem we have with seeing ourselves as saints rather than sinners is that we are painfully aware that we do sometimes sin.

It's Not Inevitable — But We Do Sometimes Go Wrong

"If we claim to be without sin, we deceive ourselves and the truth is not in us" (1 John 1:8).

You are not a sinner in the hands of an angry God. You are a saint in the hands of a loving God.

Our Fundamental Relationship With Our Heavenly Father Does Not Change When We Sin

"My dear children, I write this to you so that you will not sin. But if anybody does sin, we have one who speaks to the Father in our defence — Jesus Christ, the Righteous One" (1 John 2:1).

We Restore Harmony By Turning Back To Him And Away From Our Sin

A harmonious relationship is based on trust and obedience — when either is lacking it affects the quality of the relationship.

God Does Not Condemn Us

"Therefore, there is now no condemnation for those who are in Christ Jesus" (Romans 8:1). God is not a finger-wagging, "inspecting" kind of God. We don't need to earn our way back into His good books. We are in them already because of what Jesus has done.

Realising that you can come straight back to God in repentance when you have gone wrong and know that you are forgiven is a key to becoming a mature Christian.

PAUSE FOR THOUGHT 2

Imagine that you have fallen for a lie of the enemy and done something you know is very wrong. What is an appropriate way to behave at that point?

What can you do if, having gone wrong, you feel really condemned? (Read Romans 8:1, Hebrews 10:16-22, 1 John 1:8 – 2:2).

We Don't Have To Try To Become What We Already Are

What can I do to be accepted by God? Nothing at all! Because you are already accepted by God simply because of what Christ has done!

It is not what we **do** that determines who we **are**. It's who we **are** that determines what we **do**.

We don't need to act like we think Christians should act. We simply need to **be** who we now are: children of God.

The gospel is not about gradually becoming someone different. It starts with recognising that we **became** someone different the moment we received Christ.

 WITNESS

If you were asked by a neighbour to explain the difference between a Christian and someone who is not yet a Christian, what would you say? Do you think that a Christian is in any way better than a non-Christian? What would you say to someone who asks you, "Why should I become a Christian?"

 IN THE COMING WEEK

Read the My Father God list out loud every day. Then pick one of the truths that is particularly relevant to you and spend some time reading it in its context and asking God to help you understand it more fully.

I renounce the lie that my Father God is:	I joyfully accept the truth that my Father God is:
distant and uninterested in me.	intimate and involved (see Psalm 139:1-18).
insensitive and uncaring.	kind and compassionate (see Psalm 103:8-14).
stern and demanding.	accepting and filled with joy and love (see Romans 15:7; Zephaniah 3:17).
passive and cold.	warm and affectionate (see Isaiah 40:11; Hosea 11:3,4).
absent or too busy for me.	always with me and eager to be with me (see Hebrews 13:5; Jeremiah 31:20; Ezekiel 34:11-16).
impatient, angry or never satisfied with what I do.	patient and slow to anger and delights in those who put their hope in His unfailing love (see Exodus 34:6; 2 Peter 3:9, Psalm 147:11).
mean, cruel or abusive.	loving and gentle and protective (see Jeremiah 31:3; Isaiah 42:3; Psalm 18:2).

I renounce the lie that my Father God is:	I joyfully accept the truth that my Father God is:
trying to take all the fun out of life.	trustworthy and wants to give me a full life; His will is good, perfect and acceptable for me (see Lamentations 3:22 23; John 10:10; Romans 12:1,2).
controlling or manipulative.	full of grace and mercy, and gives me freedom to fail (see Hebrews 4:15,16; Luke 15:11-16).
condemning or unforgiving.	tender-hearted and forgiving; His heart and arms are always open to me (see Psalm 130:1-4; Luke 15:17-24).
nit-picking or a demanding perfectionist.	committed to my growth and proud of me as His growing child (see Romans 8:28,29; Hebrews 12:5-11; 2 Corinthians 7:14).

I Am the Apple of His Eye!

SESSION 3: Choosing to Believe The Truth

WELCOME

Have you had a prayer answered recently? Share the story.

Do you believe that an atheist has more or less faith than a Christian? What about a Hindu or a Muslim? What about someone who "just doesn't know"?

WORSHIP

The amazing character of our Father God (see the 'My Father God' statements from last week).

WORD

Focus verse: Without faith it is impossible to please God, because anyone who comes to him must believe that he exists and that he rewards those who earnestly seek him. (Hebrews 11:6)

Focus truth: God is truth. Find out what He has said is true and choose to believe it, whether it feels true or not, and your Christian life will be transformed.

Without Faith We Cannot Please God

Faith Is A Crucial Issue

We are saved through faith. Everywhere you look in the Bible you read that we are to walk by faith. A real, living faith is the key to success in your walk with the Lord.

Faith Is Simply Believing What Is Already True

Find out what is already true; choose to believe it whether it feels true or not, and your Christian life will be transformed.

Whether Faith Is Effective Depends On What Or Whom You Believe In

Everyone Lives And Operates By Faith

The issue of faith is not **that** we believe. Everyone believes in something or someone.

Every decision you make and practically every action you do demonstrates your faith in **something**. Believing that we are simply animals that have evolved a little higher than other animals is faith as much as any religious faith.

The Only Difference Between Christian And Non-Christian Faith Is What We Believe In

It's what or whom we believe in (the object of our faith) that determines whether our faith will be effective. It's not so much **that** we believe but **what** we believe.

That's why we only need faith as small as a mustard seed (Matthew 17:20) to move a mountain — it's not our faith that moves it, it's the One we put our faith in.

Jesus Christ Is The Ultimate Faith Object

Jesus is the one faith object that will never let us down because He "is the same yesterday and today and forever" (Hebrews 13:8).

PAUSE FOR THOUGHT 1

Do you believe that an atheist has more or less faith than a Christian? What about a Hindu or a Muslim? What about someone who 'just doesn't know'?

Tell the group about an occasion when you took God at His word – what happened?

The little boy said faith is 'trying hard to believe what you know is not true'. What do you think about the idea that 'faith is simply making a choice to believe what is already true'?

Everyone Can Grow In Faith

How Much Faith We Have Is Determined By How Well We Know The One We Put Our Faith In

Faith is making a choice to believe what God says is true and living accordingly.

"How long will you waver between two opinions? If the Lord is God, follow Him; but if Baal is God, follow him" (1 Kings 18:21).

As you try living by faith according to what God has said is true and you find that it works, you will get to know God better. Start where you are right now.

You don't **feel** your way into good behaviour — you **behave** your way into good feelings. Start by making a choice to believe the truth. Your feelings will follow in due course.

Truth

⬇

Belief

⬇

Behaviour

⬇

Feelings

PAUSE FOR THOUGHT 2

What are some of the ways our faith grows?

Can you think of a time when you asked God to do something, but you were disappointed because He didn't do it at all or didn't do it in the way you asked? What do you conclude from such difficult experiences?

Faith Grows In Difficult Times

Most of us can probably think of times when God did not do what we wanted Him to do. Sometimes we simply have to admit that our understanding of God and what we expect Him to do is simply too limited for us to know whether we are praying in accordance with His character or His will.

In order to help our faith to grow, God will often put us in a situation where we can choose whether to put our faith in Him or in something else.

God's role is to **be** truth. Our responsibility is to **believe** truth and live accordingly.

Faith Leads To Action

James 2:17-18: Faith by itself, if it is not accompanied by action, is dead. But someone will say, "You have faith: I have deeds." Show me your faith without deeds, and I will show you my faith by what I do.

People don't always live according to what they say they believe, but they will always live according to what they actually believe.

No matter what we **say**, it's what we **do** that shows what we really believe. If you want to know what you really believe, simply look at your actions.

 WITNESS

Think of someone you know who is not yet a Christian. What does the Bible say about why they don't yet believe (see 2 Corinthians 4:4, Romans 10:14-15)? Write a prayer you could pray that specifically asks God to do something about the things that are stopping them from believing. Then take God at His word and pray it!

 IN THE COMING WEEK

Every day read the Twenty 'Cans' Of Success list out loud. Then pick one of the truths that is particularly appropriate to you and make a decision to believe it regardless of feelings and circumstances. If you can find a way of stepping out in faith in some practical way based on that truth, so much the better!

1. Why should I say I can't when the Bible says I can do all things through Christ who gives me strength (Philippians 4:13)?

2. Why should I lack when I know that God shall supply all my needs according to His riches in glory in Christ Jesus (Philippians 4:19)?

3. Why should I fear when the Bible says God has not given me a spirit of fear, but one of power, love and a sound mind (2 Timothy 1:7)?

4. Why should I lack faith to fulfil my calling knowing that God has allotted to me a measure of faith (Romans 12:3)?

5. Why should I be weak when the Bible says that the Lord is the strength of my life and that I will display strength and take action because I know God (Psalm 27:1; Daniel 11:32)?

6. Why should I allow Satan supremacy over my life when He that is in me is greater than he that is in the world (1 John 4:4)?

7. Why should I accept defeat when the Bible says that God always leads me in triumph (2 Corinthians 2:14)?

8. Why should I lack wisdom when Christ became wisdom to me from God and God gives wisdom to me generously when I ask Him for it (1 Corinthians 1:30; James 1:5)?

9. Why should I be depressed when I can recall to mind God's loving kindness, compassion and faithfulness and have hope (Lamentations 3:21-23)?

10. Why should I worry and fret when I can cast all my anxiety on Christ who cares for me (1 Peter 5:7)?

11. Why should I ever be in bondage knowing that, where the Spirit of the Lord is, there is freedom (2 Corinthians 3:17; Galatians 5:1)?

12. Why should I feel condemned when the Bible says I am not condemned because I am in Christ (Romans 8:1)?

13. Why should I feel alone when Jesus said He is with me always and He will never leave me nor forsake me (Matthew 28:20; Hebrews 13:5)?

14. Why should I feel accursed or that I am the victim of bad luck when the Bible says that Christ redeemed me from the curse of the law that I might receive His Spirit (Galatians 3:13,14)?

15. Why should I be discontented when I, like Paul, can learn to be content in all my circumstances (Philippians 4:11)?

16. Why should I feel worthless when Christ became sin on my behalf that I might become the righteousness of God in Him (2 Corinthians 5:21)?

17. Why should I have a persecution complex knowing that nobody can be against me when God is for me (Romans 8:31)?

18. Why should I be confused when God is the author of peace and He gives me knowledge through His indwelling Spirit (1 Corinthians 14:33; 1 Corinthians 2:12)?

19. Why should I feel like a failure when I am a conqueror in all things through Christ (Romans 8:37)?

20. Why should I let the pressures of life bother me when I can take courage knowing that Jesus has overcome the world and its tribulations (John 16:33)?

SESSION 4: The World's View Of Truth

Part B — The World, The Flesh And The Devil

Every day the world, the flesh and the devil conspire to push us away from truth. Understanding how they work will enable us to stand firm.

WELCOME

If you could go anywhere in the world, where would you choose?

Do you think that the way you look at the world and what you believe would be very different if you had been brought up in a different culture?

WORSHIP

The uniqueness of Jesus. John 14:6, Ephesians 1:17-23, 1 Corinthians 1:30, Philippians 2:5-11.

WORD

Focus verse: Do not conform any longer to the pattern of this world, but be transformed by the renewing of your mind. Then you will be able to test and approve what God's will is — his good, pleasing and perfect will. (Romans 12:2)

Focus truth: The world we grew up in influenced us to look at life in a particular way and to see that way as "true". However, if it doesn't stack up with what God says is true, we need to reject it and bring our beliefs into line with what really is true.

What Is 'The World'?

"As for you, you were dead in your transgressions and sins, in which you used to live when you followed the ways of this world and of the ruler of the kingdom of the air." (Ephesians 2:1-2)

The world is the system or culture we grew up in and live in.

Satan is called 'the ruler of this world' (John 12:31). To a significant extent, he pulls the strings behind the world and works through it.

The World's Tactics

Tactic 1: Promising To Meet Our Deep Needs

We were created with in-built needs for security, significance and acceptance that spiritual life would have fulfilled. We instinctively looked for their fulfilment in the world which fed us its false equations (page 14).

1 John 2:15-17 helps us understand the three channels through which the world makes its appeal to us:

The Lust Of The Flesh

The more we act on the world's lies, the more unhelpful patterns of behaviour become established as "default ways of behaving".

The Lust Of The Eyes

The world presents much of its attraction through visual images. Jesus said that the eye is the 'lamp of the body' (see Matthew 6:22-23).

The Pride Of Life

The world tempts us to boast about our life based on the lie that it is our possessions or achievements that make us significant.

Tactic 2: Painting A Complete But False Picture Of Reality

We All Have A 'Worldview'

We all develop a way of looking at reality — a worldview — shaped largely by when and where we were brought up. Views of reality change but reality itself does not.

Your worldview is like a filter — you pass everything that happens around you through it in order to work out what it means. If it is faulty, it will lead you to make faulty judgments about life. Examples of some different worldviews:

1. A Non-Western Worldview: 'Animism'

- A belief that our lives are controlled by a kind of universal power and by spirits of many types.

- Need an expert to manipulate spiritual power to your advantage.

2. The Western Or "Modern" Worldview

- Divides reality into 'natural' and 'supernatural' but focuses only on the natural.
- Sees spiritual things as irrelevant to daily life.
- Reality is defined only by what we can see, touch and measure.

3. The Postmodern Worldview

- There is no such thing as objective truth.
- Everyone has their own version of "truth".
- Each person's "truth" is as valid as everyone else's.
- If you disagree with my "truth" or disapprove of my actions, you are rejecting **me.**

The Biblical Worldview : 'How It Really Is'

Truth does exist

God **is** truth

Faith and logic are not incompatible

Consider the most important question facing everybody in the world: what happens when we die?

- Hinduism teaches that when a soul dies it is reincarnated in another form.
- Christianity teaches that souls spend eternity in either heaven or hell.
- Atheists believe that we have no soul and that when we die our existence simply ends.
- Postmodernism says that you can make up whatever you want to believe as long as you don't hurt anyone else.

Does what you believe will happen to you when you die make any difference to what will actually happen? Or will all people everywhere have the same experience after death regardless of what they believed beforehand?

Logic says that we will all have the same experience regardless of what we choose to believe before the actual event.

Because God is truth, all genuine truth is His and it's true everywhere for everyone all the time no matter when and where they were born.

PAUSE FOR THOUGHT 2

Do you recognise that you have been influenced by one of the three non-Biblical worldviews we have looked at? Which one?

How different would your worldview be if you had grown up in another part of the world?

When we talk to people about Jesus' claim to be the only way to God, how can we do so without coming across as arrogant?

Tactic 3: Mix 'n' Match

We have a core belief system — our original worldview. When we become Christians, it's easy simply to add a coating of Christian beliefs to it but leave the core in place.

When push comes to shove, we revert to our core beliefs if we have never come to realise that they are not how the world really is.

"The Christian faith is not true because it works; it works because it is true... It is not simply 'true for us'; it is true for any who seek in order to find, because truth is true even if nobody believes it and falsehood is false even if everybody believes it." (Os Guinness, Time For Truth, Baker Books, 2000, pages 79-80)

PAUSE FOR THOUGHT 3

What examples can you give of how a Christian can mix and match their faith with other worldviews? Can you see tendencies to do that in your own life?

Os Guinness says 'The Christian faith is not true because it works, it works because it is true'. What measure would you use to judge whether a worldview is true?

Have you made a decision to get rid of the core beliefs the world has fed you and commit yourself to how the Bible says reality is? If so, what can you do to maintain that as you continue to live in a culture that has a different worldview?

WITNESS

How will understanding that we all grow up with a particular way of looking at the world help you as you talk to people who are not yet Christians? What will you say to those with a postmodern worldview who regard strong beliefs as a negative thing?

IN THE COMING WEEK

Ask the Holy Spirit to guide you into all truth and to reveal to your mind the lies you have believed as a result of having been brought up with a non-Biblical worldview.

SESSION 5: Our Daily Choice

WELCOME

What would you most like to do if you knew you could not fail?

WORSHIP

Worship Him for who He is.
Hebrews 13:15, Revelation 19:5, Psalm 99:9, 1 Chronicles 29:11-13.

WORD

Focus verse: You, however, are controlled not by the flesh but by the Spirit, if the Spirit of God lives in you. (Romans 8:9)

Focus truth: Although you are a new person in Christ with a completely new nature, and are free to live according to what the Holy Spirit tells you, obeying Him is not automatic.

What Did Happen When We Became Christians?

- We have a new heart and a new Spirit within us
- We have new life "in Christ"
- We have a new master (Colossians 1:13)

What Did Not Happen?

Our Body Did Not Change

Our "Flesh" Was Not Taken Away

The flesh is "the urge to do what comes naturally to a fallen human being".

It comprises thoughts that come from within us which are hostile to God and His Word but which have become our "default" ways of thinking and, therefore, behaving (see Romans 8:5-7a).

We have to train ourselves to think in a way that is in line with God's truth rather than with the flesh, a process called "renewing the mind" (Romans 12:2).

Sin Did Not Die

Sin is alive and well but we are dead to sin (Romans 6:11).

The "law of sin" is still effective. How can you overcome a law that is still effective? By a greater law: "Through Christ Jesus the law of the Spirit of life set me free from the law of sin and death" (Romans 8:2)

Our Choices

- even though we no longer have to think and react according to our flesh, we can **choose** to do so

- even though sin has no power over us, we can **choose** to give in to it

Nothing can change the fact of who we now are, and God's love for us, but the outcome of that in our day-to-day lives is down to our individual choice — are we going to choose to believe what God says is true and act on it, or not?

Three Different Types Of Person (1 Corinthians 2:14-3:3)

The Natural Person ("the man without the Spirit")
1 Corinthians 2:14 & Ephesians 2:1-3

This describes someone who is not yet a Christian:

- physically alive but spiritually dead

- separated from God

- living independently from God

- lives in the flesh; actions and choices dictated by the flesh (see Galatians 5:19-21)

- has no spiritual basis for coping with life's stresses

The Spiritual Person — 1 Corinthians 2:15

The normal state for a Christian:

- has been transformed through faith in Christ
- spirit is now united with God's Spirit
- has received forgiveness, acceptance into God's family, realisation of worth in Christ
- receives impetus from God's Spirit instead of the flesh
- is renewing the mind (ie getting rid of the old patterns of thinking and replacing them with truth)
- emotions marked by peace and joy instead of turmoil
- chooses to walk in the Spirit and therefore demonstrates the fruit of the Spirit (Galatians 5:22,23)
- still has the flesh but crucifies it daily as they recognise the truth that they are now dead to sin (Romans 6:11-14)

The Fleshly Person — 1 Corinthians 3:3

A Christian who has been made spiritually alive but, instead of choosing to follow the impulses of the Spirit, follows the impulses of the flesh.

Their daily life tends to mimic that of the natural (non-Christian) person rather than the spiritual person:

- mind occupied by wrong thoughts
- overwhelmingly negative emotions
- body showing signs of stress
- living in opposition to their identity in Christ
- feelings of inferiority, insecurity, inadequacy, guilt, worry and doubt
- tendency to get "stuck" in certain sins (Romans 7:15-24)

What is at stake is not their salvation but their fruitfulness.

In your experience, how easy is it for a Christian to act in ways that are very un-Christlike? Can you give specific examples of how you have done that yourself?

Why do you think many Christians are plagued by insecurity, inferiority, inadequacy, worry, guilt and doubt?

How can we as Christians rise above the law of sin and overcome our tendency towards sinful and selfish behaviour?

It's Down To Us!

"His divine power has given us everything we need for life and godliness through our knowledge of him who called us by his own glory and goodness" (2 Peter 1:3).

We already have "every spiritual blessing" (Ephesians 1:3)

What more does God need to do so that you can be free in Christ and be fruitful? What more does anyone else need to do?

Barriers To Growth

Ignorance

Deception (Colossians 2:6-8)

Common areas of deception:

- "this might work for others, but my case is different and it won't work for me"
- "I could never have faith like so and so"
- "God could never use me"

Unresolved Personal And Spiritual Conflicts

Sin gives the enemy a foothold (Ephesians 4:26-27), a means to hold us back. Many have come to faith but have not repented.

The Steps to Freedom In Christ are a tool you can use to examine your life and ask the Holy Spirit to show you areas where you have not repented and closed the door to the enemy's influence.

Choosing To Walk By The Spirit Is Now A Genuine Choice

Once we have committed ourselves to believe truth no matter what we feel, and we have dealt with our unresolved spiritual conflicts, we are genuinely free to make a choice every day. We can choose to obey either the promptings of flesh or the promptings of the Holy Spirit. The two are in direct opposition to each other.

We are back in the position Adam and Eve were in before the Fall, able to make a free choice.

Walking By The Spirit Is Not:

- Just a good feeling

- A licence to do whatever we want: "The flesh desires what is contrary to the Spirit, and the Spirit what is contrary to the flesh. They are in conflict with each other." (Galatians 5:17)

- Legalism: "If you are led by the Spirit, you are not under law." (Galatians 5:18)

Walking By The Spirit Is:

- True freedom: "Where the Spirit of the Lord is, there is freedom." (2 Corinthians 3:17)

- Being led: "My sheep listen to my voice; I know them, and they follow me." (John 10:27)

- Walking at God's pace in the right direction: "Come to me, all you who are weary and burdened, and I will give you rest. Take my yoke upon you and learn from me, for I am gentle and humble in heart, and you will find rest for your souls. For my yoke is easy and my burden is light." (Matthew 11:28-30)

How Can We Tell If We Are Walking By The Spirit?

Just as you can tell a tree by its fruit, you can tell whether you are walking by the Spirit by the fruit of your life (see Galatians 5:19-23).

Walking by the Spirit is a moment-by-moment, day-by-day experience. You can choose every moment of every day either to walk by the Spirit or to walk by the flesh.

But once you've understood the truth of who God is and who you are, why ever would you want to walk by the flesh any more?

PAUSE FOR THOUGHT 2

Read Galatians 3:3. As you look back on your own life, what examples can you give of times when, you now realise, you were being driven to live by your own human effort even as a Christian?

Why do you think that trying harder to do what is right isn't enough?

If we are to be led by the Spirit, how do we learn to hear and then recognise His voice?

WITNESS

How would you explain to a non-Christian the benefits of being filled with the Spirit in a way that would make sense to them?

IN THE COMING WEEK

Every day specifically commit yourself to walk by the Spirit and ask the Holy Spirit to fill you.

SESSION 6: Demolishing Strongholds

WELCOME

What is the nastiest thing anyone ever said to you or about you? Were you able to shrug it off or did it stick with you?

WORSHIP

God's grace. 1 John 3:1, Ephesians 1:6-8, John 1:16.

WORD

Focus verse: We demolish arguments and every pretension that sets itself up against the knowledge of God, and we take captive every thought to make it obedient to Christ. (2 Corinthians 10:5)

Focus truth: All of us have mental strongholds, ways of thinking that are not in line with God's truth.

What Is A Stronghold?

"It is for freedom that Christ has set us free." (Galatians 5:1)

If you're not connecting with the truth, it's probably because of mental "strongholds" and a lack of repentance.

Strongholds are connected to the flesh.

Ed Silvoso defines a stronghold as, "A mind-set impregnated with hopelessness that causes us to accept as unchangeable situations that we know are contrary to the will of God." (That None Should Perish, Ed Silvoso, Regal Books, 1994, p.155)

Neil Anderson says, "Strongholds are mental habit patterns of thought that are not consistent with God's Word."

They usually show themselves in something less than Christ-like temperament or behaviour. They also show in things we feel we should do but don't seem to be able to, or things we know we shouldn't do but don't feel able to stop. They are based on deep-rooted lies.

PAUSE FOR THOUGHT 1

Read Romans 6:1-7. The passage says we have 'died to sin' and need 'no longer be slaves to sin'. How do you feel when you experience being caught in a pattern of behaviour that you know is wrong but from which you seem unable to escape? What about when you found yourself apparently unable to do something good you knew was right?

How do you think Christians settle for a second-best Christian life?

Can you think of examples of things that were said about someone (yourself or someone else) that they can't shrug off or that stick with them all the time? Given that God is good and doesn't dangle impossible things before us, what hope do we have for change?

How Strongholds Are Established

Our Environment

The fallen world we live in is hostile to God

- we lived in it every day before we knew Christ
- we have been conditioned to conform to it

Traumatic Experiences

Eg a death in the home, a divorce or a rape. They set up strongholds because of their intensity.

If what you **believe** does not reflect truth, what you **feel** will not reflect reality.

Temptation

Strongholds are also formed or reinforced when we repeatedly give in to temptation. Every temptation is an attempt to get you to live your life independently of God. The basis for that temptation is often legitimate needs. The question is: are those needs going to be met by responding to the world, the flesh and the devil, or are they going to be met by God who promises to "meet all your needs according to his glorious riches in Christ Jesus" (Philippians 4:19)?

"Threshold Thinking"

"No temptation has seized you except what is common to man. And God is faithful; he will not let you be tempted beyond what you can bear. But when you are tempted, he will also provide a way out so that you can stand up under it." (1 Corinthians 10:13)

God has provided a way of escape from all temptation — it's right at the beginning when the tempting thought first comes into your mind. That's your opportunity to "take captive every thought to make it obedient to Christ" (2 Corinthians 10:5).

PAUSE FOR THOUGHT 2

When you are tempted and it seems impossible to overcome it, what encouragement can you take from your understanding of the Bible?

If you have given into temptation in the past, in what ways can you prepare yourself for overcoming future temptation?

Effects Of Strongholds

Faulty View Of Reality

"As the heavens are higher than the earth, so are my ways higher than your ways and my thoughts than your thoughts." (Isaiah 55:9)

"Trust in the Lord with all your heart and lean not on your own understanding. In all your ways acknowledge him, and he will make your paths straight." (Proverbs 3:5-6)

Strongholds tend to prevent us seeing what is really true because of how they make us feel.

Bad Choices

We will make better choices when we commit ourselves to know God and His ways. He really does want only the best for us and He knows what is best.

PAUSE FOR THOUGHT 3

How easy do you find it to choose to believe that what God says is true even when it doesn't feel true?

Can you think of an example of when you have done this and say what the outcome was?

Demolishing Strongholds

Do we have to put up with strongholds? No!

"For though we live in the world we do not wage war as the world does. The weapons we fight with are not the weapons of the world. On the contrary, they have divine power to demolish strongholds. We demolish arguments and every pretension that sets itself up against the knowledge of God, and we take every thought captive to make it obedient to Christ." (2 Corinthians 10:3-5)

"Check for viruses": once we deal with any foothold of the enemy, a stronghold is nothing more than a habitual way of thinking and behaving.

We need to guard our minds by "taking captive every thought to make it obedient to Christ" (2 Corinthians 10:5).

A Whole Answer

If we want a whole answer, we need to understand that we are up against not only the world and the flesh but also the devil. In the next session we will look at the role of the devil, which is, in fact, the easiest of the three to resolve.

 WITNESS

How easy do you find it to talk about Jesus to those who don't yet know Him? Do you think that any difficulty might be something to do with strongholds in your mind? Try to work out what lies might be in operation and find some truth in the Bible to commit yourself to.

 IN THE COMING WEEK

Meditate on these passages: 2 Corinthians 10:3-5; Romans 8:35-39; Philippians 4:12-13.

SESSION 7: The Battle For Our Minds

WELCOME

Has anyone ever played a really good trick on you, or have you played one on someone else?

WORSHIP

His authority — our authority. Colossians 2:15, 20, Luke 10:19, Matthew 28:18, 20, Ephesians 6:11-18.

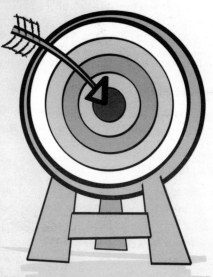

WORD

Focus verse: Put on the full armour of God so that you can take your stand against the devil's schemes. (Ephesians 6:11)

Focus truth: The battle takes place in our minds. If we are aware of how Satan works, we will not fall for his schemes.

The Battle Is Real

Jesus came to destroy the devil's work (1 John 3:8).

The tendency of those of us brought up with the Western worldview is to dismiss the reality of the spiritual world or, even if we acknowledge it, act as if it does not exist.

We are in the battle whether we like it or not. Paul tells us explicitly that we are not fighting flesh and blood but the spiritual forces of evil in the heavenly realms (Ephesians 6:10ff).

Who Is Satan?

Adam and Eve effectively handed over their right to rule the world to Satan, whom Jesus called "the prince (ruler) of this world" (John 12:31).

Satan Is Not Like God

We tend to divide the world into "natural" and "supernatural", but the Bible makes the distinction between "Creator" and "created" (see John 1:3). Like us, Satan is a created being, whereas God is the Creator. There is no comparison between them.

Satan Can Be In Only One Place At One Time

Because Satan is a created being we can infer that he can be only in one place at one time. Only God is everywhere at once.

Satan's Power And Authority Do Not Even Begin To Compare To God's

At the cross Jesus completely disarmed Satan (Colossians 2:15). Jesus is now "far above" all powers and authorities (Ephesians 1:21).

Satan Does Not Know Everything

Satan cannot perfectly read your mind. We can infer this from the Bible (eg

Daniel 2, where sorcerers using demonic powers could not read Nebuchadnezzar's mind) and from the fact that Satan is a created being and does not possess the attributes of God.

How Satan Works

Through An Organised Network Of Fallen Angels

Satan works through "rulers, authorities, powers and spiritual forces of evil in the heavenly realms" (Ephesians 6:12).

By Putting Thoughts Into Our Minds

"The Spirit clearly says that in later times some will abandon the faith and follow deceiving spirits and things taught by demons." (1 Timothy 4:1)

Three Biblical examples where Satan has put thoughts into someone's mind:

- "Satan rose up against Israel and incited David to take a census of Israel." (1 Chronicles 21:1)

- "The evening meal was being served, and the devil had already prompted Judas Iscariot, son of Simon, to betray Jesus." (John 13:2)

- "Then Peter said, 'Ananias, how is it that Satan has so filled your heart that you have lied to the Holy Spirit and have kept for yourself some of the money you received for the land?'" (Acts 5:3)

If Satan can put thoughts into our minds, he can make them sound like our own: "**I'm** useless; **I'm** ugly."

PAUSE FOR THOUGHT 1

What things have you learned about Satan so far that have surprised you? Does he seem more or less powerful than you had imagined?

How do you feel about the idea that some of the thoughts in your mind may have been put there by a deceiving spirit even though they may seem like your own thoughts? Can you identify occasions when that has happened? Are those thoughts always completely false?

Through Temptation, Accusation And Deception

If I tempt you, you know it.

If I accuse you, you know it.

But if I deceive you, by definition you don't know it.

Deception is Satan's primary strategy.

By Getting Footholds In Our Lives Through Sin

Ephesians 4:26-27 says that if you do not deal with your anger in short order, you give the devil a foothold in your life.

"If you forgive anyone, I also forgive him. And what I have forgiven — if there was anything to forgive — I have forgiven in the sight of Christ for your sake, in order that Satan might not outwit us. For we are not unaware of his schemes." (2 Corinthians 2:10-11)

Satan's greatest access to Christians is often through the sin of unforgiveness.

The Relationship Between Demons And Christians

We are not talking about Christians being "possessed", ie completely taken over or taken back by demons. At the centre of your being, your spirit is connected to God's Spirit and Satan can't have you back. We're talking about Satan gaining an amount of influence in your mind so that he can neutralise you or even use you to further his agenda.

PAUSE FOR THOUGHT 2

Read 2 Corinthians 4:4. How do you think Satan works in the lives of your non-Christian friends? Can you give examples?
What might you be able to do about this?
Read Colossians 4:2-3. How specifically might you pray for them?

Our Defence

Understand Our Position In Christ

Ephesians 1:19-22 tells us that Jesus is seated at God's right hand, the ultimate seat of power and authority, "far above all rule and authority, power and dominion".

"And God raised us up with Christ and seated us with Him in the heavenly realms in Christ Jesus." (Ephesians 2:6)

Because of the finished work of Christ, the Church is given both the power and the authority to continue His work. Our authority is to do God's will, nothing more and nothing less. We also have God's mighty power as long as we are filled (controlled) by the Holy Spirit.

Use The Resources We Have In Christ

Even though he is defeated, Satan still "prowls around like a roaring lion looking for someone to devour" (1 Peter 5:8). But we have been given resources to withstand him.

Paul tells us to put on the armour of God and stand firm (Ephesians 6:11-20).

"Submit to God. Resist the devil, and he will flee from you." (James 4:7)

This is the key for sin-confess cycles. Don't just confess but also resist the devil.

Do Not Be Frightened

Demons are petrified of Christians who know the extent of the power and authority they have in Christ.

We have no reason to be frightened of them.

"The one who was born of God keeps him safe, and the evil one cannot harm him." (1 John 5:18)

Guard Our Minds

"Prepare your minds for action." (1 Peter 1:13)

We are never told to direct our thoughts inwardly or passively but always outwardly and actively. God never bypasses our minds — He works through them.

Turn On The Light

Satan has no power over us at all unless he can deceive us into believing that he does — and we give him that power only when we fail to believe the truth.

Expose Satan's lie to God's truth, and his power is broken. "My prayer is not that you take them out of the world but that you protect them from the evil one. Sanctify them by the truth; your word is truth." (John 17:16-17)

Trying not to think negative thoughts doesn't work. As Christians we are not called to dispel the darkness. We are instructed to turn on the light.

Don't focus on the counterfeit but become intimately acquainted with the real thing. Fill your mind with positive things:

"Do not be anxious about anything, but in everything, by prayer and petition, with thanksgiving, present your requests to God. And the peace of God, which transcends all understanding, will guard your hearts and your minds in Christ Jesus. Finally, brothers, whatever is true, whatever is noble, whatever is right, whatever is pure, whatever is lovely, whatever is admirable — if anything is excellent or praiseworthy — think about such things." (Philippians 4:6-8)

PAUSE FOR THOUGHT 3

What do you think it means in practice to put on the armour of God?

If you woke up in the night with the feeling that there was a scary demonic presence in your bedroom, based on James 4:7 and what you have learned in this session, what do you think would be a good course of action?

WITNESS

How do you think Satan works in the lives of your non-Christian friends?
What might you be able to do about this?

IN THE COMING WEEK

Meditate on the following verses: Matthew 28:18; Ephesians 1:3-14; Ephesians 2:6-10; Colossians 2:13-15.

Part C — Breaking The Hold Of The Past

God does not change our past but by His grace He enables us to walk free of it. This section of the course includes going through The Steps To Freedom In Christ (see separate booklet The Steps To Freedom In Christ).

 WELCOME

Would you describe yourself as an emotional person? Tell the group about an event in the past that resulted in emotional pain or joy.

 WORSHIP

He made us so well, and He knows us so well! Psalm 139.

 WORD

Focus verse: Cast all your anxiety on him because he cares for you. Be self-controlled and alert. Your enemy the devil prowls around like a roaring lion looking for someone to devour. (1 Peter 5:7,8)

Focus truth: Our emotions are essentially a product of our thoughts and a barometer of our spiritual health.

We Can't Directly Control How We Feel

Link Between The Inner And Outer Person

Our inner person (soul/spirit) was designed to function in union with our outer person (our body). The obvious correlation is between the brain and the mind.

The brain functions like computer hardware. The mind is like the software. In the Bible the overwhelming emphasis is on the mind: choosing truth, believing the truth, taking every thought captive, and so on.

What We Can And Cannot Control

We cannot directly control our emotions but we can change them over time as we change what we **can** control: what we believe and how we behave.

Our Feelings Reveal What We Really Believe

Our emotions are to our soul what our ability to feel pain is to our body.

If what you **believe** does not reflect truth, then what you **feel** will not reflect reality. Life's events don't determine who you are or what you feel — it's your perception of those events.

The more we commit ourselves to the truth and choose to believe what God says is true, the more we will see our circumstances from God's perspective and the less our feelings will run away with us.

Changing How We Feel

A major cause of stress is that we have come to believe through past experiences or failures that we are helpless or hopeless.

But no Christian is helpless or hopeless. Healing comes by recognising and believing what is actually already true.

PAUSE FOR THOUGHT 1

What do you think of the statement, 'it is not your circumstances that determine how you feel, but rather how you see those circumstances'?

If you are prone to being overwhelmed by negative emotions, how can you start looking at things in a healthier way and aligning yourself with the truth of God's Word?

If you struggle with your emotions, why not create a 'Spiritual First Aid Kit' to help you? The idea is that you collect together several things that you know you will find helpful when you find yourself feeling vulnerable and have them ready for use whenever necessary. These will be things that will point you towards the truth such as a key verse to read, someone you can call, a written-out prayer to pray, a favourite book or passage from a book, or favourite praise music. Write the items in the gaps below.

MY SPIRITUAL FIRST AID KIT

Following Feelings Makes Us Vulnerable To Attack

You don't **feel** your way into good behaviour. You **behave** your way into good feelings. We start by choosing to believe the truth which works itself out in our behaviour. This then over time leads to a change in our feelings.

Truth ➡ Belief ➡ Behaviour ➡ Feelings

A failure to handle emotions such as anger (see Ephesians 4:26-27) and anxiety (see 1 Peter 5:7-9) in the right way sets us up for problems.

Three Ways To Handle Emotions

Cover It Up (Suppression)

Suppression is when we consciously ignore our feelings or choose not to deal with them. It's unhealthy and dishonest.

Explode (Indiscriminate Expression)

Indiscriminate expression is unhealthy for those around us — see James 1:19,20.

Be Honest (Acknowledgment)

The healthy response is to be honest and acknowledge how we feel, first to God but also to others.

PAUSE FOR THOUGHT 2

When something triggers strong emotions in you, how do you tend to handle it?

Read Psalm 109:6-15. Does it surprise you that something like that is in the Bible? Remember, this is the holy, inspired, perfect word of God! Have you ever felt that strongly about someone else? How did you respond? Why is it important to tell God what you really feel about your circumstances?

s there anything you could tell God that He does not already know?

We can approach issues in our lives focusing either on truth or on feelings. If we start with the truth in God's Word and choose to believe it it will work out in our behaviour and ultimately into our feelings. But if we start with feelings, we'll be led to a very different conclusion. Listed below are three examples of situations we may face followed by a table that shows the likely outcome if we start with truth and a table showing what might happen if we start with feelings. Do you think that they are realistic?

A. When I face a real challenge, I can see it either as a chance to trust God and grow or as too much to handle.

B. When people seem cool towards me, I can either trust God for favour or feel uncertain how to act around them.

C. When I face financial pressure, I can either see it as an opportunity to grow in faith and prove God's faithfulness or feel anxious.

Truth Orientated (Top to Bottom) Approach

	TRUTH	BELIEF	BEHAVIOUR	FEELINGS
A	God will never leave me on my own (Isaiah 43:2,3)	God won't put me through more than I can bear and I can trust Him to help me	Positive approach to the challenges	Confident God will help me
B	If God is for me who can be against me (Romans 8:31)	I am going to trust God in this relationship	I will overlook slights and be affirming of others	Confident God will give me favour as I need it
C	I have been giving faithfully according to my means and God has promised to meet my needs (Philippians 4:19)	Expect him to do so	Approach expectantly and do what I can to increase income and reduce expenditure	Peace and confidence

Feelings Orientated (Bottom to Top) Approach

	FEELINGS	BEHAVIOUR	BELIEF	MY VIEW OF REALITY
A	Overwhelmed by the demands on me. Exhaustion. I can't cope. Depression.	Dip out. Run away.	I am helpless	I am a perennial failure
B	I feel unwanted, rejected	React at the first sign of a slight (real or imagined) or back off from people	I am unlovable and people hate me	As people don't want to be around me, I resent and criticise them and become grumpy and irritable
C	Anxious about money	Striving to get money, or stinginess	It is all down to me to make money	I can't make it happen – anger; I made it happen – pride

Handling Past Traumas

God doesn't want emotional pain from our past to influence us negatively today.

We remain in bondage to the past, not because of the trauma itself, but because of the lies we believed at the time. These lies stay with us and become strongholds.

Children of God are not primarily products of their past. They are primarily products of Christ's work on the cross and His resurrection. Nobody can fix our past, but we can be free from it. We can re-evaluate our past from the perspective of who we are now in Christ. God sets us free as we forgive from our hearts those people who have offended us.

 WITNESS

If you are feeling angry, anxious or depressed, do you think it would be better not to let that show to non-Christians around you? Why? Why not?

 IN THE COMING WEEK

Consider the emotional nature of the Apostle Peter. First, have a look at some occasions where he let his emotions run away with him and acted or spoke too hastily: Matthew 16:21-23; Matthew 17:1-5; John 18:1-11. Second, look at how Jesus was able to look beyond these emotional outbursts and see his potential: Matthew 16:17-19. Finally, see how that came true when Peter, under the power of the Holy Spirit, became the spokesperson of the early church: Acts 2:14-41. Nothing in your character is so big that God cannot make something good out of it!

SESSION 9: Forgiving From The Heart

 WELCOME

Read Matthew 18:21-25 or act it out using the script on pages 74 and 75. Then try to put yourself in the place of one of the characters and say what strikes you most about the story.

 WORSHIP

His complete forgiveness of us. Hebrews 4:16, Ephesians 3:12, Psalm 130:1-5.

 WORD

Focus verse: In anger his master turned him over to the jailers to be tortured, until he should pay back all he owed. This is how my heavenly Father will treat each of you unless you forgive your brother from your heart. (Matthew 18:34-35)

Focus truth: In order to experience our freedom in Christ, we need to relate to other people in the same way that God relates to us — on the basis of complete forgiveness and acceptance.

The Need To Forgive

"If you forgive anyone, I also forgive him. And what I have forgiven — if there was anything to forgive — I have forgiven in the sight of Christ for your sake, in order that Satan might not outwit us. For we are not unaware of his schemes." (2 Corinthians 2:10-11)

Nothing keeps you in bondage to the past more than an unwillingness to forgive.

Nothing gives Satan greater opportunity to stop a church growing than roots of bitterness which are caused by personal unforgiveness.

It Is Required By God (Matthew 6:9-15)

We must learn to relate to others on the same basis that God relates to us.

It Is Essential For Our Freedom (Matthew 18:21-35)

God does not want His children to languish in bitterness and be bound to the past.

The Extent Of Our Own Debt

We need to understand the extent of our own debt.

Those who have been forgiven much love much. Those who have been forgiven little love little (see Luke 7:47).

Our best is like filthy rags before God (Isaiah 64:6). Without Christ we all stand condemned. We have all been forgiven much.

Repayment is impossible

Ten thousand talents was a huge sum. Just like our debt to God, it was impossibly large.

Mercy is required

Justice = giving people what they deserve
Mercy = not giving people what they deserve
Grace = giving people what they don't deserve

We are to relate to others in exactly the same way that God relates to us.

PAUSE FOR THOUGHT 1

People sometimes feel their sins weren't 'that bad' or as bad as other people's. What do you think?

How much have you been forgiven? Little or much? Why do you think that?

So That No Advantage Can Be Taken Of You (2 Corinthians 2:10-11)

The word Jesus used for "torture" in Matthew 18:34 usually refers to spiritual torment in the New Testament (eg Mark 5:7).

If we do not forgive, we open the door to the enemy's influence.

What Does It Mean To Forgive From The Heart?

Jesus warns that, if you do not forgive from your heart, you will suffer some kind of spiritual torment.

We recommend a formula: "**Lord, I choose to forgive** (name the person) **for** (specifically what they did or failed to do) **which made me feel** (verbally tell the Lord every hurt and pain He brings to your mind)".

Forgiveness must be extended to others (Ephesians 4:31-32). However, the crisis is only between God and us.

We Forgive To Stop The Pain

It is for our own sake that we forgive. We think that by forgiving someone we let them off the hook — but by not forgiving them we stay hooked to the pain and the past.

PAUSE FOR THOUGHT 2

What, if anything, have you heard so far that is new to you?

Naturally speaking none of us would want to remember past hurts. Why do you think it is necessary to do so in order genuinely to forgive? If you disagree, why?

We have seen that the crisis of forgiveness is between you and God rather than between you and the person who hurt you. Why does it often not feel that way?

Why is it that, if there is no forgiveness, it is not the offender but the offended who continues to feel pain?

What is Forgiveness?

Not Forgetting

You can't get rid of a hurt simply by trying to forget it. We do, however, choose never again to bring up the offence and use it against the person.

Not Tolerating Sin

It is perfectly possible to forgive but still take steps to put an end to ongoing abuse by removing yourself from a situation or calling in the authorities.

Not Seeking Revenge

Forgiveness is not sweeping what was done under the carpet. It is simply taking a step of faith to hand it over to God who is the righteous judge and will demand payment for what was done. (See (Romans 12:19)

Resolving To Live With The Consequences Of Sin

Everybody is living with the consequences of somebody else's sin. The only real choice we have is to do that in the bondage of bitterness or the freedom of forgiveness.

Forgiveness is to set a captive free and then realise that you were the captive!

PAUSE FOR THOUGHT 3

How has this session changed your view of what forgiveness is or is not?

Next time someone offends you, how quickly do you think you will forgive?

If you forgive, will you ever get justice for what was done to you? How?

WITNESS

How might this question of forgiveness challenge someone who is not yet a Christian? Are there any ways you can demonstrate forgiveness to someone who does not yet know God?

IN THE COMING WEEK

Ask the Holy Spirit to prepare your heart by leading you into all truth and starting to reveal to you the areas you will need to bring into the light when you go through The Steps To Freedom In Christ.

Characters:	Peter, Jesus, Servant 1, Servant 2, Master
Peter	Lord, how many times shall I forgive my brother when he sins against me? Up to seven times?
Jesus	I tell you, not seven times, but seventy-seven times.
	Therefore, the kingdom of heaven is like a king who wanted to settle accounts with his servants. As he began the settlement, a man who owed him ten thousand talents was brought to him. Since he was not able to pay, the master ordered that he and his wife and his children and all that he had be sold to repay the debt.
	The servant fell on his knees before him.
Servant 1	Be patient with me, and I will pay back everything.
Jesus	The servant's master took pity on him, cancelled the debt and let him go. But when that servant went out, he found one of his fellow servants who owed him a hundred denarii. He grabbed him and began to choke him.
Servant 1	Pay back what you owe me!

Jesus	His fellow servant fell to his knees and begged him:
Servant 2	Be patient with me, and I will pay you back.
Jesus	But he refused. Instead, he went off and had the man thrown into prison until he could pay the debt. When the other servants saw what had happened, they were greatly distressed and went and told their master everything that had happened.
	Then the master called the servant in.
Master	You wicked servant, I cancelled all that debt of yours because you begged me to. Shouldn't you have had mercy on your fellow servant just as I had on you?
Jesus	In anger his master turned him over to the jailers to be tortured, until he should pay back all he owed.
	This is how my heavenly Father will treat each of you unless you forgive your brother from your heart.

As you go through Step 3 (Forgiveness) of The Steps To Freedom In Christ, you are encouraged to pray as follows for each person you need to forgive: "Lord, I choose to forgive (name the person) for (what they did or failed to do), which made me feel (verbally tell the Lord every hurt and pain He brings to your mind)".

Use this page to record the things you say after "which made me feel". Some of them will reveal mental strongholds that you can work on. Session 10 will equip you with a strategy for this.

SESSION 10: Walking in Freedom Every Day

Part D — Growing As Disciples

Having taken hold of our freedom in Christ, we now want to grow to maturity. In this section we will learn how to stand firm, how to relate to other people and how to stay on the path of becoming more like Jesus.

WELCOME

How did you find The Steps To Freedom In Christ process?

WORSHIP

He has set me free!
Galatians 5:1, Psalm 119:45.

WORD

Focus verse: But solid food is for the mature, who by constant use have trained themselves to distinguish good from evil. (Hebrews 5:14)

Focus truth: Our success in continuing to walk in freedom and grow in maturity depends on the extent to which we continue to renew our minds and train ourselves to distinguish good from evil.

Growing To Maturity

Our normal state should be one of growth towards spiritual maturity but it's all too easy to become an old Christian without necessarily being a mature one! (See 1 Corinthians 3:1-3)

The Difference Between Freedom And Maturity

"His divine power has given us everything we need for life and godliness through our knowledge of him who called us by his own glory and goodness." (2 Peter 1:3 — see also Ephesians 1:3 and Colossians 2:9-10)

We already have **everything we need** to become mature Christians but it does not happen automatically.

There is a great difference between freedom — which can be obtained in a relatively short time — and maturity, which is the work of a lifetime.

Maturity is a **process** of growth. Freedom, however, is a **position we take** in response to Christ's victory over sin and Satan. We are either free or bound in various areas of our lives. We don't grow into freedom in these areas: we take possession of freedom by the authority we have in Christ wherever we realise that we have been deceived and bound.

But if we do not first take hold of our freedom, we cannot move on to maturity.

Three Keys To Maturity

1. Taking Personal Responsibility

God has set things up in a certain way and has decreed that some things are His responsibility and some things are our responsibility. He will not do for us what is ours to do. Neither God — nor anyone else — can repent for us, believe for us or forgive for us because those things are for us to do.

If you want to move on as a Christian, it's your responsibility. No one else can do it for you.

How can a Christian be transformed? "By the renewing of your mind" (Romans 12:2). Whose responsibility is that? Yours!

The key to your transformation is in your hands. Nothing and no one can prevent you from becoming the person God wants you to be — except you! That's great news!

You alone can do it — but you can't do it alone. We do need other people to encourage us, love us and support us, but ultimately we are each responsible for our own relationship with God.

PAUSE FOR THOUGHT 1

If Christians have not grown as quickly as they might have, what sort of things may have hindered them? How do you feel about your own rate of growth?

2 Peter 1:3 tells us that we already have everything we need to live the Christian life (see also Ephesians 1:3 and Colossians 2:9-10). Why do you think that sometimes doesn't feel true?

Do you agree with the phrase, "You alone can do it... But you can't do it alone"? When it comes to growing to maturity as a Christian, what are some of the things that are the individual Christian's personal responsibility to do? How can other Christians encourage them?

2. Renewing Our Minds

Having resolved personal and spiritual conflicts using The Steps To Freedom In Christ, you may well be finding that you are able to connect with what is really true more easily. However, we still have the flesh which includes those "default", unhelpful ways of thinking based on lies. These are strongholds but we have weapons to deal with them (see 2 Corinthians 10:4-5).

Dealing With Lies — "Stronghold-Busting"

1. Determine the lie you have been believing (any way you are thinking that is not in line with what God says about you in the Bible). In doing this, ignore what you feel but commit yourself wholeheartedly to God's truth.

2. Find as many Bible verses as you can that state the truth and write them down.

3. Write down what effects believing the lie has had in your life.

4. Write a prayer or declaration based on the formula:

   I renounce the lie that...

   I announce the truth that...

5. Finally, read the Bible verses and say the prayer/declaration every day for 40 days.

Note: there are some examples on pages 84-86 (but if you can, it's better to create your own rather than take a ready-made one).

PAUSE
FOR THOUGHT 2

LIES EXERCISE: Look at the list below of typical lies that people come to believe about themselves. Can you find some Bible verses that show that those things cannot be true of any Christian? Write them in the "Truth" column.

LIES	TRUTH
Unloved	
Abandoned	
Rejected	
Inadequate	
Hopeless	
Stupid	
Ugly	

Can you identify a lie that you have been believing? Perhaps some became apparent as you went through The Steps To Freedom In Christ – there may have been a recurring theme of belief that you know is a lie but keeps feeling true, e.g. 'I am a failure', 'I am helpless', 'I am unworthy', 'I know this works for others but it won't work for me'.

Write down the lie and what the specific outcome of believing it is in your life. Then think of at least two or three Bible verses that counter the lie. Finally write out 'I renounce the lie that' and 'I announce the truth that'. Use it every day for the next six weeks or so.

3. Taking A Long-Term View

Renewing our mind takes time and effort. There is no 'quick fix'. But you can have every expectation of tearing down strongholds as you commit yourself every day to the truth in God's Word.

Train Yourself To Distinguish Good From Evil

"But solid food is for the mature, who by constant use have trained themselves to distinguish good from evil." (Hebrews 5:14)

When we are intimately acquainted with the truth, we will instantly recognise a counterfeit.

Run The Race

"Forgetting what is behind and straining towards what is ahead, I press on towards the goal to win the prize for which God has called me heavenwards in Christ Jesus. All of us who are mature should take such a view of things." (Philippians 3:13b-15a)

We need to commit ourselves to the race for the long-term. Know where you are going — spiritual maturity — and keep running towards it.

Other Practical Steps

- Read 'Walking In Freedom by Neil Anderson
- Accountability relationship
- Find support if you are working through past traumas
- Do this teaching again!

PAUSE FOR THOUGHT 3

Write down the practical steps you are going to take to maintain your freedom and continue to renew your mind.

 WITNESS

Write down the two most important things you have learned on this course so far. How do you think you could explain them to a not-yet Christian?

 IN THE COMING WEEK

Work out a stronghold-buster for the most significant lie you have uncovered and start going through it.

The lie: that overeating brings lasting comfort.

Effects in my life: harmful to health; getting overweight; giving the enemy a foothold; stopping my growth to maturity

Proverbs 25:28: Like a city whose walls are broken down is a man who lacks self-control.

Galatians 5:16: So I say, live by the Spirit, and you will not gratify the desires of the flesh.

Galatians 5:22: But the fruit of the Spirit is love, joy, peace, patience, kindness, goodness, faithfulness, gentleness and self-control. Against such things there is no law. Those who belong to Christ Jesus have crucified the flesh with its passions and desires.

2 Corinthians 1:3-4: Praise be to the God and Father of our Lord Jesus Christ, the Father of compassion and the God of all comfort, who comforts us in all our troubles, so that we can comfort those in any trouble with the comfort we ourselves have received from God.

Psalm 63:4-5: I will praise you as long as I live, and in your name I will lift up my hands. My soul will be satisfied as with the richest of foods; with singing lips my mouth will praise you.

Psalm 119:76: May your unfailing love be my comfort.

Lord, I renounce the lie that overeating brings lasting comfort. I announce the truth that you are the God of all comfort and that your unfailing love is my only legitimate and real comfort. I affirm that I now live by the Spirit and do not have to gratify the desires of the flesh. Whenever I feel in need of comfort, instead of turning to foods I choose to praise you and be satisfied as with the richest of foods. Fill me afresh with your Holy Spirit and live through me as I grow in self-control. Amen

Tick off the days:								
1	2	3	4	5	6	7	8	9
10	11	12	13	14	15	16	17	18
19	20	21	22	23	24	25	26	27
28	29	30	31	32	33	34	35	36
37	38	39	40					

The lie: that I am abandoned and forgotten.

Effects in my life: withdrawing from others; thinking people don't like me; seeming aloof; frightened

Deuteronomy 31:6: Be strong and courageous. Do not be afraid or terrified because of them, for the LORD your God goes with you; he will never leave you nor forsake you.

Isaiah 46:4: Even to your old age and grey hairs I am he, I am he who will sustain you. I have made you and I will carry you; I will sustain you and I will rescue you.

Jeremiah 29:11: "For I know the plans I have for you," declares the LORD, "plans to prosper you and not to harm you, plans to give you hope and a future."

Romans 8:37-38: For I am convinced that neither death nor life, neither angels nor demons, neither the present nor the future, nor any powers, neither height nor depth, nor anything else in all creation, will be able to separate us from the love of God that is in Christ Jesus our Lord.

Dear Heavenly Father
I renounce the lie that I am abandoned and forgotten and will be left on my own.
I announce the truth that you love me, that you have plans to give me a hope and a future and that absolutely nothing can separate me from your love.
In Jesus' name. Amen

Tick off the days:								
1	2	3	4	5	6	7	8	9
10	11	12	13	14	15	16	17	18
19	20	21	22	23	24	25	26	27
28	29	30	31	32	33	34	35	36
37	38	39	40					

The lie: that I cannot resist the temptation to look at internet porn.

Effects in my life: deep sense of shame; warped sexual feelings; unable to relate to other people as God intended; harmful to my marriage

Romans 6:11-14: In the same way, count yourselves dead to sin but alive to God in Christ Jesus. Therefore do not let sin reign in your mortal body so that you obey its evil desires. Do not offer the parts of your body to sin, as instruments of wickedness, but rather offer yourselves to God, as those who have been brought from death to life; and offer the parts of your body to him as instruments of righteousness. For sin shall not be your master, because you are not under law, but under grace.

1 Corinthians 6:19: Do you not know that your body is a temple of the Holy Spirit?

1 Corinthians 10:13: No temptation has seized you except what is common to man. And God is faithful; he will not let you be tempted beyond what you can bear. But when you are tempted, he will also provide a way out so that you can stand up under it.

Galatians 5:16: So I say, live by the Spirit, and you will not gratify the desires of the flesh.

Galatians 5:22: But the fruit of the Spirit is love, joy, peace, patience, kindness, goodness, faithfulness, gentleness and self-control.

I renounce the lie that I cannot resist the temptation to look at internet porn. I declare the truth that God will always provide a way out when I am tempted and I will choose to take it. I announce the truth that if I live by the Spirit — and I choose to do that — I will not gratify the desires of the flesh and the fruit of the Spirit, including self-control, will grow in me. I count myself dead to sin and refuse to let sin reign in my body or be my master. Today and every day I give my body to God as a temple of the Holy Spirit to be used only for what is right. I declare that the power of sin is broken in me. I choose to submit completely to God and resist the devil who must flee from me now.

Tick off the days:								
1	2	3	4	5	6	7	8	9
10	11	12	13	14	15	16	17	18
19	20	21	22	23	24	25	26	27
28	29	30	31	32	33	34	35	36
37	38	39	40					

SESSION 11: Relating To Others

WELCOME

What is the thing that has struck you the most on this course so far?

WORSHIP

Praising God for those people He has given us. 1 John 3:16.

WORD

Focus verse: Jesus replied: "'Love the Lord your God with all your heart and with all your soul and with all your mind.' This is the first and greatest commandment. And the second is like it: 'Love your neighbour as yourself.' All the Law and the Prophets hang on these two commandments." (Matthew 22:37-40)

Focus truth: As disciples of Christ we must assume responsibility for our own character and seek to meet the needs of others, rather than the other way round.

Understanding Grace

We love because He first loved us (1 John 4:19).

We give freely because He gave freely to us (Matthew 10:8).

We are merciful because He has been merciful to us (Luke 6:36).

We forgive because He forgave us. (Ephesians 4:32).

Our Responsibilities To Others

"Who are you to judge someone else's servant? To his own master he stands or falls. And he will stand, for the Lord is able to make him stand." (Romans 14:4)

"Do nothing out of selfish ambition or vain conceit, but in humility consider others better than yourselves. Each of you should look not only to your own interests, but also to the interests of  others. Your attitude should be the same as that of Christ Jesus." (Philippians 2:3-5)

We are responsible for our own **character** and meeting the **needs** of others.

Being Aware Of Our Own Sins

When we see God for who He is, we don't become aware of the sin of others, but of our own sin. However, when we are lukewarm in our relationship with God, we tend to overlook our own sin and see the sin of others.

Focus On Responsibilities Rather Than Rights

In every relationship we have both rights and responsibilities — but where should we put the emphasis?

Do husbands have a right to expect their wives to be submissive to them? Or do they have a responsibility to love their wives as Christ loved the Church?

Do wives have a right to expect their husbands to love them? Or do they have a responsibility to love and respect their husbands who in turn have the responsibility of being the head of the home?

Do parents have a right to expect their children to be obedient? Or do they have a responsibility to bring them up in the training and instruction of the Lord, and to discipline them when they are disobedient?

Does being a member of a local church give you the right to criticise others? Or does it give you a responsibility to submit to those in authority over you and relate to one another with the same love and acceptance you have received from Christ?

When we emphasise our rights above our responsibilities in any relationship we sow the seeds of destruction.

Learning not to focus constantly on the failings of others and choosing to think well of them is so much easier in the long run than always feeling let down and badly treated.

PAUSE FOR THOUGHT 1

How would you sum up our responsibility to other people?

Why do you think we have a tendency to judge others and look out for our own needs?

If you find yourself becoming critical of others and unaware of your own shortcomings, what might the problem be and what can you do to put it right?

What About When Others Do Wrong?

Everyone finds it difficult to own up to sin.

Playing the role of the Holy Spirit in another person's life won't work.

Discipline Yes, Judgment No

"Do not judge, or you too will be judged. For in the same way as you judge others, you will be judged, and with the measure you use, it will be measured to you." (Matthew 7:1)

"Brothers, if someone is caught in a sin, you who are spiritual should restore him gently." (Galatians 6:1)

We are told not to judge, but we are to carry out discipline.

Judgment is always related to **character** whereas discipline is always related to **behaviour**.

Calling somebody "stupid", "clumsy", "proud" or "evil" is an attack on their **character** and it leaves them with no way forward.

But if you point out someone's sinful **behaviour**, you are giving them something that they can work with: "You are right; what I just said wasn't true, and I am sorry."

Discipline And Punishment Are Not The Same

Punishment looks backwards, whereas discipline looks forwards.

God's discipline is a proof of His love and is designed to bring a "harvest of righteousness" (Hebrews 12:5-11).

The point of discipline is not to punish someone but to help them become more like Jesus.

When We Are Attacked

"When they hurled their insults at him, he did not retaliate. When he suffered, he made no threats. Instead, he entrusted himself to him who judges justly." (1 Peter 2:23)

If you are wrong, you don't have a defence. If you are right, you don't need one. Christ is your defence.

Authority And Accountability

From which end of this list (top or bottom) did God first come to you?

Authority

Accountability

Affirmation

Acceptance

"While we were still sinners, Christ died for us" (Romans 5:8). Acceptance came first, and then the affirmation: "The Spirit himself testifies with our spirit that we are God's children" (Romans 8:16).

If authority figures demand accountability without giving acceptance and affirmation, they will never get it.

PAUSE FOR THOUGHT 2

Why is it unwise to try to be another person's conscience? What can happen if we try?

What are the differences between judgment, punishment and discipline?

The next time someone attacks or accuses you, what would be a good response?

Should We Express Our Needs?

If we have needs in a relationship that are not being met, it is important that we let people know what they are. However, a need must be stated as a need, and not as a judgment.

We Reap What We Sow

God has placed us in community because that is how we grow. Every one of us needs to be loved, accepted and affirmed. Those are legitimate needs.

Jesus said, "It is more blessed to give than to receive" (Acts 20:35). We cannot sincerely help somebody else without helping ourselves in the process.

"Give and it will be given to you. A good measure, pressed down, shaken together and running over, will be poured into your lap. For with the measure you use, it will be measured to you." (Luke 6:38)

If you want somebody to love you, love somebody. If you want a friend, be a friend.

People are unreasonable, illogical and self-centred.
Love them anyway.
If you do good, people will accuse you of selfish, ulterior motives.
Do good anyway.
If you are successful, you will win false friends and true enemies.
Succeed anyway.
The good you do today will be forgotten tomorrow.
Do good anyway.
Honesty and frankness make you vulnerable.
Be honest and frank anyway.
The biggest people with the biggest ideas can be shot down by the smallest people with the smallest minds.
Think big anyway.
People favour underdogs but follow only top dogs.
Fight for the underdog anyway.
What you spend years building may be destroyed overnight.
Build anyway.
People really need help, but may attack you if you help them.
Help people anyway.
Give the world the best you've got and you'll get kicked in the teeth.
Give the world the best you've got anyway.

PAUSE FOR THOUGHT 3

What legitimate needs do we all have and how can we express those needs without it backfiring on us?

What do you think is wrong with the following statements? How could they be said better?

"You always leave me to do the clearing up after dinner and go and watch the TV. You are so selfish and lazy."

"Your room is a disgrace. It is always such a mess! You are a real slob. I pity the person you marry."

WITNESS

How can you be a good neighbour to those who live on your street? How could you get to know them better, so that you would have a better idea of what their needs are?

IN THE COMING WEEK

Read Luke 6:27-41. This session may have convicted you of the need to relate differently to your family, friends, and neighbours. You might want to seek the forgiveness of others. If you sense the Lord's conviction, then go to that person or persons and ask their forgiveness, stating clearly that what you have done is wrong. (Don't do this by letter or e-mail — it might be misunderstood or used against you.)

SESSION 12: Where Are You Heading?

WELCOME

What would you like to do before the end of your life?

WORSHIP

He will be with us always. Hebrews 13:5,6; Psalm 94:14; Matthew 28:20.

WORD

Focus verse: The goal of this command is love, which comes from a pure heart and a good conscience and a sincere faith.
(1 Timothy 1:5)

Focus truth:
Nothing and no
one can keep us
from being the
person God
created us to be.

Your Christian Walk Is The Result Of What You Believe

We have all come to believe that certain things will give us satisfaction, significance, fun, etc. But will they actually deliver the goods or are the goals we have developed faulty in some way?

In this session we use the term "goal" to refer to those outcomes we have come to believe are fundamental to our sense of who we are, those results by which we measure our very selves.

Feelings Are God's Red Flag of Warning

God has equipped us with a feedback system that is designed to grab our attention so that we can check the validity of the direction we're heading in: our emotions.

When an experience or relationship leaves us feeling angry, anxious or depressed, those emotional signposts are there to alert us to the possibility that we may be working towards a faulty goal which is based on a wrong belief.

Anger Signals A Blocked Goal

If you don't want to be angry, get rid of any goal that can be blocked by other people or circumstances that you have no right or ability to control.

Anxiety Signals An Uncertain Goal

Depression Signals An Impossible Goal

We can, of course, be depressed for biochemical reasons but, if there is no overriding physical cause, then depression is usually rooted in a sense of hopelessness or helplessness because we have goals that seem impossible to achieve.

PAUSE FOR THOUGHT 1

How, if at all, do our emotions indicate whether our goals are in line with God's will?

How do people typically respond to blocked goals? What has been your tendency when you don't get your own way or when someone or something is keeping you from doing what you want?

Depression is often the result of a sense of helplessness or hopelessness, particularly concerning perceptions of the future, circumstances around us and our view of ourselves. How can those perceptions (beliefs) be overcome by faith in God?

Wrong Responses When Our Goals Are Frustrated

If we believe that our sense of worth is dependent on other people and circumstances, we will try to manipulate those people and circumstances.

Turning Bad Goals Into Good Goals

If God has a goal for your life, can it be blocked, or is its fulfilment uncertain or impossible? No!

No God-given goal can, therefore, be dependent on people or circumstances that we have no right or ability to control.

What do we do with a goal whose fulfilment is in itself a good thing but which depends on events or circumstances that we cannot control? We need to downgrade it in our thinking from a goal, upon which our whole sense of who we are depends, to what we might call "a Godly desire".

The Difference Between A "Goal" And A "Desire"

A Godly **goal** is any specific orientation that reflects God's purpose for your life and does **not** depend on people or circumstances beyond your ability or right to control.

A Godly **desire** is any specific result that **does** depend on the cooperation of other people, the success of events or favourable circumstances which you have no right or ability to control.

The crucial difference is that you cannot base your success or sense of worth on your desires, no matter how Godly they may be, because you cannot control their fulfilment.

However, the only person who can block a Godly goal or make it uncertain or impossible is you.

God's Goal For Our Lives

2 Peter 1:3-10 starts by telling us what has already been done for us:

- we have everything we need for life and godliness
- we participate in God's nature
- we have escaped the corruption in the world

If you try to live out your Christian life without understanding what has already been done for you, you will simply be "trying harder". God's goal for our lives is based on what has already been done by Christ.

"For this very reason, make every effort to add to your faith goodness; and to goodness, knowledge; and to knowledge, self-control; and to self-control, perseverance; and to perseverance, godliness; and to godliness, brotherly kindness; and to brotherly kindness, love." (2 Peter 1:5-8)

This is a list of character attributes. God's primary concern is not so much what we **do** but what we're **like**. His goal for us is to do with our character.

The goal that God has for any Christian could be defined as: to become more and more like Jesus in character.

Difficulties Help Us Towards The Goal

"We rejoice in our sufferings, because we know that suffering produces perseverance; perseverance, character; and character, hope." (Romans 5:3-4)

"Consider it pure joy, my brothers, whenever you face trials of many kinds, because you know that the testing of your faith develops perseverance. Perseverance must finish its work so that you may be mature and complete, not lacking anything." (James 1:2-4)

The difficulties we face are actually a means of achieving our supreme goal of becoming more like Jesus in character. Persevering through difficulties results in improved character.

We need occasional mountain top experiences but the fertile soil for growth is always down in the valleys, not on the mountain tops.

PAUSE FOR THOUGHT 2

What benefits do you see for our freedom and emotional well-being from differentiating between Godly goals and Godly desires?

What is God's primary goal for your life? Why can this never be blocked?

Why can it be so liberating to know that nothing and no one can keep you from being the person God created you to be?

When Our Goal Is Love

Paul says, "The goal of our instruction is love" (1 Timothy 1:5) (NASB). Love is the character of God, because God is love (1 John 4:7,8).

If you make Godly character your primary goal then the fruit of the Spirit that will be produced in your life is love: anger gives way to patience; anxiety to peace; and depression to joy.

 WITNESS

How can distinguishing between goals and desires help you to be a more effective witness?

 IN THE COMING WEEK

Take some time to evaluate your faith by completing the "What Do I Believe?" questionnaire on page 102 of the Participant's Guide.

You will not be asked to share how you are doing with the rest of the group. Give some serious thought as to how you would complete the sentences.

	Low				High

1. How successful am I?   1   2   3   4   5

I would be more successful if ....

2. How significant am I?   1   2   3   4   5

I would be more significant if..

3. How fulfilled am I?   1   2   3   4   5

I would be more fulfilled if..

4. How satisfied am I?   1   2   3   4   5

I would be more satisfied if...

5. How happy am I?   1   2   3   4   5

I would be happier if...

6. How much fun am I having?   1   2   3   4   5

I would have more fun if..

7. How secure am I?   1   2   3   4   5

I would be more secure if..

8. How peaceful am I?   1   2   3   4   5

I would have more peace if...

WELCOME

Has anyone ever deceived you into believing something that turned out to be untrue?

WORSHIP

Praising God that He is able to complete the work He started in us! Philippians 1:6; Jude 24.

WORD

Focus verse: I am not saying this because I am in need, for I have learned to be content whatever the circumstances. I know what it is to be in need, and I know what it is to have plenty. I have learned the secret of being content in any and every situation, whether well fed or hungry, whether living in plenty or in want. I can do everything through him who gives me strength. (Philippians 4:11-13)

Focus truth: If we want to be truly successful, fulfilled, satisfied, etc, we need to uncover and throw out false beliefs about what those things mean and commit ourselves to believing the truth in the Bible.

For To Me To Live Is....

Paul says, "For to me, to live is Christ and to die is gain" (Philippians 1:21).

But:

- For to me to live is my career, to die is..... loss.
- For to me to live is my family, to die is.... loss.
- For to me to live is a successful Christian ministry, to die is.... loss.

When the goal of our life is simply Christ and becoming like Him in character, when we die it just gets better!

What Do I Really Believe?

The "What Do I Believe?" questionnaire on page 102 will help you understand what you actually believe. Right now you are living by faith according to what you actually believe. The question is, are your beliefs about what will bring you success, significance etc. in line with what God says?

The further we go in our Christian walk, the more important it is to make sure our belief system is based on what is really true.

Success Comes From Having The Right Goals

God's goal for your life begins with who you are on the basis of what God has already done for you (see 2 Peter 1:3-10).

We start with what we believe (faith). Our primary job then is diligently to adopt God's character goals — goodness (moral excellence), knowledge, self-control, perseverance, godliness, brotherly kindness and Christian love — and apply them to our lives. Focusing on God's goals will lead to success in God's terms.

Reaching God's goals is not dependent on other people or talents, intelligence or gifts. Every Christian can know who they are in Christ and grow in character.

For Joshua, success hinged entirely on one thing: whether or not he lived according to what God had said (Joshua 1:7,8).

Success is accepting God's goal for our lives and by His grace becoming what He has called us to be.

Significance Comes From Proper Use Of Time

What is forgotten in time is of little significance. What is remembered for eternity is of great significance.

"If any man's work... remains, he shall receive a reward." (1 Corinthians 3:14, NASB)

"Train yourself to be godly. For physical training is of some value, but godliness has value for all things, holding promise for both the present life and the life to come." (1 Timothy 4:7,8)

If you want to increase your significance, focus your energies on significant activities: those that will remain for eternity.

Fulfilment Comes From Serving Others

"Each one should use whatever gift he has received to serve others, faithfully administering God's grace in its various forms." (1 Peter 4:10)

Fulfilment is discovering our own uniqueness in Christ and using our gifts and talents to build others up and glorify the Lord.

The key is to discover the roles we occupy in which we cannot be replaced, and then decide to be the person God wants us to be in those roles.

Satisfaction Comes From Living A Quality Life

"Blessed are those who hunger and thirst for righteousness, for they shall be filled." (Matthew 5:6)

Satisfaction is a quality issue, not a quantity issue. The key to personal satisfaction is not found in doing more things but in deepening our commitment to quality in the things that we are already doing.

Satisfaction comes from living righteously and seeking to raise the level of quality in our relationships and in what we do.

Happiness Comes From Wanting What We Have

The world's concept of happiness is having what we want. Yet true happiness is wanting what we have.

"Godliness with contentment is great gain. For we brought nothing into the world, and we can take nothing out of it. But if we have food and clothing, we will be content with that." (1 Timothy 6:6-8)

If we focus on what we don't have, we'll be unhappy. If we begin to appreciate what we already have, we'll be happy all our lives.

Fun Comes From Enjoying Life Moment By Moment

Fun comes from throwing off inhibitions and being spontaneous. The secret is to remove unbiblical hindrances such as keeping up appearances.

It is a lot more fun pleasing God than people.

Security Comes From Focusing On Eternal Values

We feel insecure when we depend upon things that we have no right or ability to control. We will feel secure when we focus on eternal values.

Jesus said no one can snatch us out of His hand (John 10:27-29) and Paul declared that nothing can separate us from the love of God in Christ (Romans 8:35-39). How much more secure can you get than that?

Every "thing" we now have we shall some day lose. Jim Elliot said, "He is no fool who gives what he cannot keep to gain that which he cannot lose." See also Philippians 3:7,8.

Peace Comes From Quieting The Inner Storm

If we look for peace in external circumstances we will be disappointed.

The peace of God is internal, not external.

Peace **with** God is something we already have (Romans 5:1). The peace **of** God is something we need to take hold of every day in our inner person.

We can have the internal peace of God even in the midst of storms that rage in the external world.

"My peace I give you. I do not give to you as the world gives. Do not let your hearts be troubled and do not be afraid." (John 14:27)

It's The First Day Of The Rest Of Your Life

Walking by faith comes down to making a decision every day to believe what God says is true and living accordingly by the power of the Holy Spirit.

You can leave here in the sure knowledge that:

- you are God's child and He delights in you.
- whatever your current circumstances, He is intimately concerned in your life and has plans to give you hope and a future (Jeremiah 29:11).
- nothing and no one can prevent you from becoming the person God wants you to be — it hinges solely on your decision to adopt God's goal for your life.
- it's about what you're **like** more than what you **do**.

This was written by someone (of unknown source) who decided to take God at His word:

I am part of the "Fellowship of the unashamed". I have Holy Spirit Power. The die has been cast. I've stepped over the line. The decision has been made. I am a disciple of His. I won't look back, let up, slow down, back away, or be still. My past is redeemed, my present makes sense, and my future is secure. I am finished and done with low-living, sight-walking, small-planning, smooth knees, colourless dreams, tame visions, mundane talking, miserly giving, and dwarfed goals!

I no longer need pre-eminence, prosperity, position, promotions, plaudits, or popularity. I don't have to be right, first, top, recognised, praised, regarded or rewarded. I now live by presence, lean by faith, love by patience, lift by prayer and labour by power.

My face is set, my gait is fast, my goal is heaven, my road is narrow, my way is rough, my companions few, my guide reliable, my mission clear. I cannot be bought, compromised, detoured, lured away, turned back, diluted or delayed. I will not flinch in the face of sacrifice, hesitate in the presence of adversity, negotiate at the table of the enemy, ponder at the pool of popularity, or meander in the maze of mediocrity.

I won't give up, shut up, let up or burn up till I've preached up, prayed up, paid up, stored up and stayed up for the cause of Christ.

I am a disciple of Jesus. I must go till He comes, give till I drop, preach till all know, and work till He stops.

And when He comes to get His own, He'll have no problems recognising me. My colours will be clear.

What we do for God won't be to earn His approval or prove ourselves. It will be simply because we love Him, because He first loved us.

The rest of your life is ahead of you. You can become the person God wants you to be. Nothing and no one can get in your way!

PAUSE FOR THOUGHT 2

If happiness is 'wanting what you have' rather than 'having what you want', how can you change your thinking about your situation?

Fun may be fleeting, but the joy of the Lord lasts forever. How can you experience the joy of the Lord and make your Christian experience more fun?

What causes people to feel insecure? How can you be more secure?

For individual reflection. Write down two of the eight areas in the 'What Do I Believe?' questionnaire which are the most challenging to you. How can you make progress in those areas?

WITNESS

Pick two or three of the eight areas we have considered. How would not-yet-Christians around you be affected if you were to put the principles into practice?

IN THE COMING WEEK

Work out which of the eight areas in the 'What Do I Believe?' questionnaire are the most challenging for you. Spend some time reading the relevant passages for those areas in "God's Guidelines for the Walk of Faith" on the following page. You could use them to develop a stronghold-buster for the ongoing renewing of your mind.

Success comes from having the right goals

Success is accepting God's goal for our lives and by His grace becoming what He has called us to be (Joshua 1:7,8; 2 Peter 1:3-10; 3 John 2).

Significance comes from proper use of time

What is forgotten in time is of little significance. What is remembered for eternity is of greatest significance (1 Corinthians 3:13; Acts 5:33-40; 1 Timothy 4:7,8).

Fulfilment comes from serving others

Fulfilment is discovering our own uniqueness in Christ and using our gifts to build others up and glorify the Lord (2 Timothy 4:5; Romans 12:1-18; Matthew 25:14-30).

Satisfaction comes from living a quality life

Satisfaction is living righteously and seeking to raise the quality of our relationships and the things we do (Matthew 5:5; Proverbs 18:24; 2 Timothy 4:7).

Happiness comes from wanting what we have

Happiness is being thankful for what we do have, rather than focusing on what we don't have — because happy are the people who want what they have! (Philippians 4:12; 1 Thessalonians 5:18; 1 Timothy 6:6-8).

Fun comes from enjoying life moment by moment

The secret is to remove unbiblical hindrances such as keeping up appearances (2 Samuel 6:20-23; Galatians 1:10, 5:1; Romans 14:22).

Security comes from focusing on eternal values

Insecurity comes when we depend on things that will pass away rather than things that will last for ever (John 10:27-30; Romans 8:31-39; Ephesians 1:13,14).

Peace comes from quieting the inner storm

The peace of God is internal, not external (Jeremiah 6:14; John 14:27; Philippians 4:6,7; Isaiah 32:17).

Become A Friend Of Freedom In Christ!

If you are excited about the effect the Freedom In Christ course can have on individuals, churches and communities, you can be involved in making that impact even greater. We'd love to have you in the team!

Freedom In Christ Ministries exists to equip the Church worldwide to make fruitful disciples. We rely heavily for financial support on people who have understood how important it is to give leaders the tools that will enable them to help people become fruitful disciples, not just converts.

Friends of Freedom In Christ commit to giving a regular monthly sum to us. In return, we keep you fully up-to-date with what we are doing and how your money is being used.

Typically your support will be used to:
- help us equip UK church leaders
- help people overseas establish national Freedom In Christ offices
- translate our material into other languages
- partner with other organisations worldwide to equip leaders
- develop further training and equipping resources

Please send your completed form to Freedom In Christ, PO Box 2842, READING RG2 9RT or sign up at www.ficm.org.uk. Thank you!

- -

Title:_____ First Name:_____ Surname:_____

Address:_____

_____Postcode:_____ Phone:_____

E-mail:_____

❑ I enclose a one-off gift of £_____

❑ I have set up a standing order for: ❑£100   ❑£50   ❑£20   ❑£____
per month to Freedom In Christ Ministries
(Sort Code: 60-17-21 Account number: 54191653)

GIFT AID (please complete if you pay UK tax)*. I am a UK taxpayer and wish Freedom In Christ Ministries to treat all donations I make as Gift Aid Donations.

Signature:_____ Date:_____

*Please note that you must pay an amount of income or capital gains tax equal to or greater than the tax we reclaim on your donations. Please remember to inform us of any change in your tax status. Freedom In Christ Ministries is a registered charity no. 1082555.